Tips for Reading Together

This book contains two stories: *The Red Hen* (page 3) and *Tip Top* (page 17).

- Talk about the title and the picture on the front cover and the title pages of each story.

- Find the letters *e* and *i* in these titles and talk about the sounds they make when you read them in these words.

- Look at the *e*, *o*, *a*, *i* and *ss* words on pages 4 and 15. Say the sounds in each word and then say the word (e.g. *T-e-ss*, *Tess*).

- Read the stories and find the words with the letters *e*, *o*, *a*, *i* and *ss* in them.

- Do the fun activities at the end of each story.

Children enjoy re-reading stories and this helps to build their confidence.

Have fun!

After you have read *The Red Hen*, find ten feathers in the pictures.

The main sounds practised in this book are 'e' as in *hen*, 'o' as in *pot*, 'a' as in *bag*, 's' as in *Tess*, and 'i' as in *tin*.

For more hints and tips on helping your child become a successful and enthusiastic reader look at our website www.oxfordowl.co.uk.

The Red Hen

Written by Roderick Hunt
Illustrated by Nick Schon,
based on the original characters
created by Roderick Hunt and Alex Brychta

OXFORD
UNIVERSITY PRESS

Read these words

hen	pen
net	Tess
not	got
box	pot

Tess the hen was not in the pen.

Dad had a net.

Mum had a bag.

Tess ran.

Mum ran and Dad ran.

Chip did not run.

Chip got a big box.

He set the box up.

He put in a pot.

Chip got Tess in the box.

Dad put Tess in the pen.

Talk about the story

What did Mum use to try to catch Tess?

What did Chip do to catch Tess?

Why did Tess go under the box?

How do you help out at home?

Missing letters

Put in the missing letter to make the word.

e a o

h__n   p__n

b__g   n__t

g__t   p__t

Spot the difference

Find the five differences in the two pictures.

Tip Top

Written by Roderick Hunt
Illustrated by Nick Schon,
based on the original characters
created by Roderick Hunt and Alex Brychta

OXFORD
UNIVERSITY PRESS

Read these words

big	tin
bin	tip
wok	top
box	on

Kipper had a big box.

He put a wok on top.

Kipper put a bin on the wok.

He put a tin on the bin.

Kipper set a jug on the tin.

He put a pan on the jug.

Kipper put a mug on the pan,

It will tip!

24

and he set Ted on top.

It did tip!

Talk about the story

What did Kipper put on the tin?

What did Kipper put on the pan?

Why did the tower tip?

What have you used to build towers? Did your tower tip?

What's in the picture?

What are the things in the picture that have *e* and *u* in the middle of the word? Find something in the picture that has *a* in the middle of the word. Find the three things that have *u* in the middle of the word.

pan; mug, jug, mum

Spot the difference

Find the five differences in the two pictures.

Maze

Help Chip get to Tess.

Read with Biff, Chip and Kipper offers two important pathways to learning to read. **First Stories** have been specially written to provide practice in reading everyday language, and the **Phonics** stories help children practise reading by decoding sounds in words, as they learn to do in school.

Books at Level 2: Starting to read

Look out for the next level: Becoming a reader

OXFORD
UNIVERSITY PRESS

Great Clarendon Street, Oxford OX2 6DP
Text © Roderick Hunt 2007
Illustrations © Alex Brychta and Nick Schon 2007
First published 2007. This edition published 2011
Series Advisors: Kate Ruttle, Annemarie Young

British Library Cataloguing in Publication Data available
ISBN: 978-0-19-279460-4
10 9 8 7 6 5 4 3 2
Printed in China by Imago
The characters in this work are the original creation of Roderick Hunt and Alex Brychta who retain copyright in the characters.